I AM A BODY OF LAND

SHANNON WEBB-CAMPBELL

WITH AN INTRODUCTION BY LEE MARACLE

I AM
A BODY
OF LAND

Book*hug Press
2019

The production of this book was made possible through the generous assistance of the Canada Council for the Arts and the Ontario Arts Council. Book*hug Press also acknowledges the support of the Government of Canada through the Canada Book Fund and the Government of Ontario through the Ontario Book Publishing Tax Credit and the Ontario Book Fund.

Book*hug Press acknowledges the land on which it operates. For thousands of years it has been the traditional land of the Huron-Wendat, the Seneca, and most recently, the Mississaugas of the Credit River. Today, this meeting place is still the home to many Indigenous people from across Turtle Island, and we are grateful to have the opportunity to work on this land.

LIBRARY AND ARCHIVES CANADA CATALOGUING IN PUBLICATION

Title: I am a body of land / Shannon Webb-Campbell ; with an introduction by Lee Maracle.
Names: Webb-Campbell, Shannon, 1983– author. | Maracle, Lee, editor.
Description: Poems.
Identifiers: Canadiana (print) 20190046198 | Canadiana (ebook) 20190046465 | ISBN 9781771664776 (softcover) | ISBN 9781771664783 (HTML) | ISBN 9781771664790 (PDF) | ISBN 9781771664806 (KINDLE)
Classification: LCC PS8645.E225 I2 2019 | DDC C811/.6—DC23

Printed in Canada

For anyone finding their way home

(Unresolved)
"Trauma is unspeakable" —Kali Tal

Table of Contents

Introduction

MY PUBLISHERS PHONED ME AND SAID they were in trouble; they had a writer whose manuscript had problems. They had spent a great deal on it and so had little resources left to hire me to remedy the situation. I listened to their trouble and agreed to work on it. Artists in this country come from a sexist, colonial, and racialized culture. These spill into our consciousness and sometimes drown out the voices of our spirit, the desires of our heart, and fog up whatever clarity we came with when we approached our computers, easels, and so forth. No one escapes. All we can do is challenge each other, own it, transform it, and move on.

This is a complex process. First, there is the business of understanding the art form you are playing with, in this case poetry. I am not the winner of any poetry prize. I write poetry about things that do not make for good poetry. I then must learn more than the next person learns about poetry and work more diligently with its particular and sometimes peculiar parameters. It is easy to overstep the boundaries of fairness, sharing, and decency in any art form, and I choose not to critique any of the foregoing, but there must be clarity and the poet must stay poetic. Poets overstep the boundaries more often than I care to admit. I do recall reading a poem that had a line in it: "Fucking Cariboo Squaws." Instead of getting all in a knot about the racism, I looked at the line itself. Where is the image, where is the emotionality, where is the spirit? It is a stereotype. Those who write in stereotypes presume that the image must have existed at one time and that the picture hadn't changed in the early days of the gold rush, miners subjected Cariboo women to mass rape. Reinventing this wound one hundred years later as historic poetry is just plain racist, and, of course, that is hurtful. Lesson: always look for the current image. Dodge the stereotype.

I am handling this rework of Shannon's poetry, so first I decide to go after the image. Make sure we are not dancing on the edge of a stereotype or immersing ourselves in it. To do that I need to assess the level of belief that Shannon has in me as a guide. If it is low, I will have to re-dig inside my poetic toolbox and sharpen my wits. I have several conversations with her. My second daughter often talks about Canadian passive-aggressive behaviour as a national trait. She means that Canadians will agree with you, then five minutes later come up with a new argument against you; they will re-present your story so that it includes the sort of evidence that falls short of what you actually said, and begin the argument anew—a passive agreement followed by an aggressive, collective gang fight.

"I spoke to my elder last night," Shannon begins, "and he said I am entitled to speak Mi'kmaw anytime I want. It is my language."

"Yes, you are," I answered, "but your elder is not a poet; they likely don't know that if a line looks imageless and arrogant it is bad poetry and that you do have permission to write bad poetry, but publishers don't have to gamble on it. If you are using an

Indigenous language to show off, then it is bad poetry. Poetry speaks to the soul. It can be sharp as a knife, quick and stinging, or soft as a feather, but always it is humble to the language in which the poetry is written. It is not about what words we want to use or which language we want to speak, it is about what we want the reader to see, to feel, and to experience. Nothing else matters."

In that sense, the poet is secondary to the mission. This is a trap. I know this trap. It is a good one. You lock yourself in and have to write yourself out. The poem is not satisfied until it has outsized, outspoken, and outwitted you—clarified you. What we get from this is the power of moving through the obstacles to our own spirit's growth.

Raven likes shiny stuff
The mirror lays in the grass
Raven pecks at it
Pecks at it until it isn't shiny
*Raven is disappointed**

Picking at shiny stuff until it is not shiny anymore is entitlement without power.

We are working away, one poem at a time, when Jay lets us know we are running out of time. I think this is a Book*hug trait. I haven't been publishing with them for long and it has already happened twice. Okay. I ask Shannon to bring all the rest of her poems to my porch next week and we will go through them. She worries about time; I assure her we will be fine. Not sure why she believed me, but in retrospect, it does not really matter. I think I am a good teacher. Others think so too; they also compare me

---

* From an oral story.

variously to a running buffalo herd, a truck, and other various mean metaphors for things that can run over the fragile egos of authors, nearly crushing them, but they believe they learned a lot from me. The writers I teach often win awards.

My daughter hears Shannon groan from the porch. "Welcome to my world. She does this to everyone," she laughs. "I have been through it," and she laughs some more.

I see revising poetry as similar to developing film: you stick it in the chemical bath, shake it up until you begin to see the image, then slowly shake it, carefully, until the image is clear. Do not give it another shake. Then you grab it and throw it into a fixing bath and give it a couple of passes, then hang it out to dry. Chemical baths are rough, shaking is no fun, but I do not see any other way to get through revising this book of poems in a day.

Thank goodness Shannon is amenable and easy to work with. She has many questions, but that is because she wants to get it. She does not want to be sitting on this porch revising her poetry ever again.

Line by line, stanza by stanza, and poem by poem. I search for the gold standard in her work. The gold standard is a line that is impossibly beautiful and rich with spiritual and intellectual fruit. Dripping with it. It tries to elude me, but finally I find it. It is there. I see it. It is in the line that makes me want to weep. I want to weep for the image, for the moment, for my soul, for Shannon's, and I know this is what she can do.

"I am a body of land."

She can scale these heights. Make her dig around for it, I tell myself. Do not settle for anything less.

Conocimiento, Gloria Anzaldua wrote: the way we know.

"What do you want the reader to see?" I ask. Shannon stares blankly, starts some kind of sociological explanation. I stop her and repeat: "What do you want the reader to see?" This question has an answer. She knows the answer and I need to hear it. The answer tells me how I will recognize her gold standard, and so I press on. I am a tad merciless about this part of the process. I feel us crashing through this river of images, our breath fighting for common understanding. We catapult along in the rapids, and at the same time we head for the open sea. I love this journey, not sure that Shannon does, but in the end, she says she "got it," and I breathe. Okay. We have a book, three and a half weeks and one day on the porch.

There are controversies surrounding this book. I am not going to talk about them here. They no longer matter. I wanted Shannon and I to turn this book into a work that belonged solely to the author. No stereotypes, no inappropriate cultural flag-waving. I wanted a book that reflected the author's spirit, her yearnings, her trials, and her desires. I believe we accomplished that. I believe that had I scolded her, argued with her right to say this or that, we would never have gotten anywhere. The process begins with respect. We do not have to respect our adversaries, those whom we consider "Other," but if we do respect them, they will surprise us. We came together on my porch: my daughter, Shannon, and myself. All three of us learned something, and we diminished the need for Othering one another. I love when that happens.

Revising and editing poetry is never about correcting anything—it is about falling into the poem, and both of us playing with it until it is clear, unbundled, and poignant. Pick up the gems that are there uncut and unrefined and not necessarily as shiny as

I AM A BODY OF LAND

After the Upheaval

I've landed here
my voice damp with shame
my insides burn
I wait for someone to ask me to leave

I'm a translation of a translation
somewhere on the chopping block
of cutting and absence I cower
I trace tree lines

I am looking for a root
a stem to grow a sense of who I am
metabolize where I come from
and process who I belong to

I'm afraid of all that came before

I Have Been Called Out

I don't know my community
I don't belong
I have no spirit name
I am a question of authenticity

I'm still here
tangled up with the colonists
unpacking the settler within
I try not to disappear

I Want to Embrace My Ancestors

voices of father, my aching mother
my grandfather who cried out from the orphanage
deafens me to my grandmothers

I cannot find my way back to the circle
I'm spinning out a feral tether, a loose end

A Sphere Within Our Sphere

try different entry points,
avert your suffering eyes,
and intersect with love.

the body of this book is
traumatized.
the body is a wound.
we collapse on trauma's floor.
we stand in the spine of
what comes after.

Somewhere Beyond Known Body and Spirit

at an intersection between sex and rape
love and abuse—I hear whispers

Make room for violence
for the abusers and manipulators

generations move within
I enter spirit world
wade through lifetimes of shame
a mix of voices sing
clouds of smoke layered the lodge
like smoke the pain peels back
layer by layer

I Looked to the River

skinny-dipping under moonlight
I found myself in brackish water
floating on my back as dusk loomed.

Nipples perked toward stars
only mountain shadows watched.
My body became silk
as I swam across Conne River.

By Reclaiming Ktaqamkuk

bound by stories, myth
and misconceptions
we honour all who came before
who are here now
and who will come after.

On Airplane Mode

I fly west to outsmart
the seduction of harm.
If I'm far enough away
you can no longer reach me.

Seven months not talking
echoes of colonization run deep.
Be careful with this story you now live.

The Call-Out Was a Cry Out

Every hour I hear your voice like bells repeating—
you are alone in this, no one will stand with you.
I tried to speak but your ears don't hear.

You called me out when I needed to be
called in. Your grandmothers and my grandmothers
gave us more than this. You say I'm not
Indian enough, like I don't already know.

Block, obsess, threaten
—we no longer share our complex histories.
Separated by the telling,
a divide that repeats pain,
we can no longer see ourselves.

I Feed Myself Poems

I stop puking up 5,000 years long enough to swallow them

    I bathe in freshwater to cleanse my body and spit all this out

        I wake from lazy nightmares
                    with your hands on my face

          I cry in muffles for the healer with your
                       fingers in my mouth

      I try to sing lullabies but the language does not come

      I say a prayer to become the dream if you will be the catcher

                We used to share a table.

Runaway

"What makes you think I'm enjoying being led to the flood?
We got another thing coming undone"
                                        —*The National*

as life shifts and orbits
into another transition,
book a flight
to go back home.

Islands make islanders,
fly into the inter-nation between
lunar eclipses.

See How Low the Moon Hangs

when stars touch cliffs
land moves closer to sky
to meet earth's breath

return to where water
outweighs land. between
feral bog and the ocean's expanse
find remedy to temper your heart's fury

big skies heave shades of grey
winds howl their own voice

love needs truth and witness
no hesitations, always a spare room
to gather lifetimes and generations.

I Only Have One Photo Left of Mary

for Mary Webb

No taller than wildflowers, with hands tucked into a soiled apron,
her hair covered. She looks into a lens with eyes that know
what plants are medicines, and which roots hold poisons.

In still-life photograph, Mary grew gardens, picked berries.
She distilled the moon's shine, pickled harvests, and *kept* meat.
Taught her youngsters to skin rabbits, make liquor blind.
Never drink the old stuff, she said.

Whenever I drink, or my moon bleeds, I think of Mary,
who travelled to women's wombs by dog team,
horses, sometimes even snowshoes.

Don't matter how many days it took,
or what storm railed down home,
she took medicines with her, bleached bloody bodies.
Mary always got there in time for the baby.

Grandmother went to the hospital sick in '78,
kept praying for young ones to grow old,
help them help those who carry on when she goes.
Mary died five years and four days before I got born
yet something inside me calls for her.

Their World View Is a
New Home in an Ancient Land

if you think you can hold dominion over flora and fauna,
that a body and life can be property,
you'd better try buying a constellation.

I am not landless, nor law.
in sorrow's aftermath remind me—
I am a body of land unlearning
what cannot be expressed.
Dig to find a physical knowing, ceremony.

Our cells remind us, we are living
in the intersection of trauma and desire
—a disordered state.

How can we imagine ourselves not broken?
Set vowels and variables.
Open to seven generations before and after.

I Carry You Through Water

swimming with a blind woman
wearing a yellow swim cap, in the slow
lane. Her Seeing Eye dog sits on the edge
of a public pool half-asleep on deck,
one eye cocked, watching us splash in chlorinated water.

A Hot Pink Sky

shifts into spirit realm as cities gather
to flash-mob round-dance in your name,
five decades after you arrived.

You are now flying into the wingspan home,
listening to earthbound songs from a bird's-eye view.
May you find your shoes to dance again.

We Slipped Through the Cracks of a System

found kin sharing Sonic Youth earbuds,
down creek from our suburban houses
where you still sing Junkie's Promise.
We lit up a garden of maple leaves,
stood in the lands of vapour,
watched mercury turn solid.

You called this the meeting place.

You Fear Retribution

You know trauma lives
You unearth
You retell
You harness
You unflinch power
Your throat carries bodies
You call on the sky
You sing the ancestors forward
You are not divided from your body
You are not separate from earth
You know the land will outlast us all

Newfoundland is where the colonization of North America began, and the colonial agenda still prevails. Yet long before John Cabot arrived in 1497 and claimed the land on behalf of England, the Mi'kmaq, Innu, Inuit, and Beothuk were the traditional custodians of Newfoundland and Labrador's lands and waters. Despite this history—or perhaps because of it—the Indigenous people of Newfoundland and Labrador have long been dismissed and shamed into silence. When the province joined Confederation in 1949, the government, under premier Joey Smallwood's guidance, inaccurately declared that there were "no Indians on the island of Newfoundland." Smallwood's dismissal prevented the formal and legal recognition of Newfoundland's Indigenous people for decades.

On Receiving a Government Letter Rejecting Our Indian Status

Father calls, says they are revoking us
his voice gravel thick

a deadweight of shame returns
thousands of papers board a plane
soar through the sky to land
like scalps on doorsteps of would-be Qalipu

my ancestors are on trial
we no longer live in No'Kmaq Village
mark Smallwood's infamous words
there are no Indians on the island of Ktaqamkuk

denial repeats to eradicate Mi'kmaq existence
one too many anglicized names
spin webs of displaced identity

Goddamn Jackatars
government commands colonial amnesia
you do beadwork in the suburbs
google Mi'kmaq translations
only learned to bang your drum far from home

Ottawa notes I'm not Indigenous enough
still landless, no claim, no bones to hone
Father says it was good for a while
but what about the next seven generations

I tell him, *L'nu Neuptjeg.*
I'm Mi'kmaq forever.

I Used to Take the Gum from Your Mouth

when you passed out drunk
halfway up the stairs,
hung over a staircase
on Northern Dancer Boulevard

afraid you'd choke
to death on Dentyne,
I'd chew cinnamon-fused hops
before spitting leftover gum into the toilet

I knew you'd hate to let a corporation
have your last fired breath

Letter to Joseph R. Smallwood

after Marilyn Dumont's "Letter to Sir John A. Macdonald"

Dear Joey: I'm still here and mixed
Mi'kmaq after all these years.
you're long dead, yet
confederation couldn't stop
Newfoundland's ongoing
colonial violence.
you continued so unapologetically,
telling Ottawa there are no red Indians
Nancy April, we killed them all.
and you know, Joey,
after all your declarations
bowing to the settlers,
we're still here, we remain
Mi'kmaq despite stolen status cards,
none of us landless,
all of us Caribou.

Elegy Revised

I am an edge walker
        I am a frozen seabird dumped on a beach
                I am a beach walker who came upon a heap of
                    bloodied turrs

I am a murre who is graceless on land but swims like a fish
        I plunge 600 feet into the water before I am shot down
mid-flight
                I am the only hunter allowed to kill seabirds
around here

I am an interpretive site where the Beothuk used to roam
        I live on a rez where the only way in is the only way out
                        I am a verdict

  I am a taddler who speaks to newspapers
        I am a country that questions the nature of abuse
I am a failed legal system

                I am a medicine woman who lost her medicines
        I am a stolen prayer
                I am a blurred vision

I am turning a blind eye
        I am jealousy's root system
                I am dishonouring my father's sobriety

I am an empty bottle under the sink
       I am swallowing all the tears that now live in my body
             I am a woman unprotected like our waterways

             I am a teenage girl just starting puberty
     I am not someone who wants you to forget any of this
        I am a boreal river where we can no longer swim

Outside the Prison

a guard watches.
She is cautious of burning matches.
Snow starts drifting outside. Inside we
lock together to write letters.

You Told Me You Were a Hunter

spelled out your strategy:
you choose prey from afar, observe
never approach from behind.

You make sufferers weak
circle and lure
until you're invited in—
this is how you capture.

You devour women's bodies
leave spirit-remains
for lesser animals
mark skins with your scent
go back into the woods
skulking for others.

I watch closely
examine how you pull back
control every muscle
hardly exhale before
you approach slowly.

I catch you off guard
come up from behind
tackle body to earth
nip at ears

make you howl
salvaging all hides
skinned before mine.

I Was Only Young

when father left
the moon left sky
so the stars guided me home

I started drinking
carte blanche on the liquor cabinet
I wet the bed
the shame stays with me

when my voice stopped working
my hands took over

The Powwow at the Edge of the World

I walk with Father on the grounds
when all the dancers are gone
I am told by many that I must let go
forgive what I don't know

He talks of that summer at the powwow
where all our relations were dancing
how this land is somewhere he could never live

Another Litany

You are near first light yearning. You are looking to heal. You can't find sleep. You are awake with the wind. You are trying to unlearn harm. You are promised mercy. You finally hear star speak. You will dream of her. Your grandmothers will catch your fear. You are praying for a safe return.

If Love Is Our Last Hope the Medicine Wheel Is Our Compass

look north to catch midnight
find death in winter

look east for dawn
find light in spring

look south at birth
find rebirth in summer

look west at dusk
find wisdom in fall

each direction: a spirit helper
an element, a sacred medicine

a circle embodies the passage of sun
and four seasons. I am of the dawn
here at the edge, knowing first light
you know longer shades of day

look to animal stars
find sweetgrass

look for mineral sun
find tobacco

look at plant moon
find cedar

look to human earth
find sage

our lives move in circles
we are sun-wise

The Antelope's Wife

a found poem from Louise Erdrich's The Antelope's Wife

Earth and sky touch
everywhere and nowhere
like sex between strangers.
There is no definition
and no union is assured.

If you chase that line
it will retreat from you
at the same pace you set.
Heart pounding,
air burning in your chest.

Only humans see that line
as an actual place.
But like love, you'll never
get there. You'll never
catch it. You'll never know.

A Hyperactive Text

I'm too tired to be self-reflexive. This isn't post reflexivity. I am the reader. I am the page. I am told nostalgia is no longer valuable. We are living in a trauma state, our capital is your pain. No one wants to admit to feminism's nostalgia. We are the post riot grrrrrls trying not to pretend we're over it. I bow to nostalgia. The academic and intellectual work is no longer hysterical. I am no longer in hysterics. I am producing novelty. Academe tells me I am living in a post colonial body. I'm a politic and required reading. I am practising decolonial love. I am fucking myself with prototypes, and reporting back to the manufacturers. I've been to the neocraft, heart exploding like pink fun fur and disco balls. I'm still sleeping in your forgotten feminist histories. I am a secret meaning expressing no value. I am in the cells of all living things. I am a new kind of readership. I am the author lying. I am a poem talking about my categorical breakdown. I am an idea that precedes the text. I am reading post poetry. I am before a spoken language. I am made of men and words. I am made from women and the body. I am a metaphor for the avant-garde. I am a boundary object. I am the author reading. I am post thinking about death. I am taking away from humanness. I am power in the hands of readers. I am a post romantic lyric poet. I am meaning versus intention. I am post etymology. I am animal vulnerability. I am a collision of colonialism and war.

The-o-ry Crit-i-cal

This is post revolution
This is post potential
This is post theory
This is post queernesss
This is post activism
This is post marxism
This is post art
This is post acknowledging the land
This is post unceded
This is post unsurrended
This is post territory
This is post commodification
This is post white guilt
This is post settler
This is post consent
This is post privilege
This is post capital
This is post imagination
This is post segregation
This is post validation
This is post racism
This is post sexism
This is post heterosexism
This is post classism
This is post violence
This is post emotional wounding

This is post jazz
This is post gaslighting
This is post cultural relation
This is post homage
This is post bad faith
This is post self-deception
This is post silencing
This is post routine violence
This is post unpredictable
This is post harm
This is post routine
This is post rape
This is post freedom
This is post reason
This is post emotion
This is post cultural production
This is post essentialism
This is post have been there
This is post haven't been there
This is post reinterpretation
This is post coming of age
This is post transformative
This is post seeing yourself in the world
This is post archive
This is post belatedness
This is post taboo
This is post questions
This is post process
This is post practice

This is post marginal voices
This is post bacterium
This is post history of writing
This is post humanism
This is post product
This is post cycle
This is post meaning
This is post nourishment
This is post slippage
This is post difference
This is post symbiosis
This is post boredom
This is post process
This is post body
This is post human centre
This is post abstraction
This is post decomposition
This is post drug
This is post irony
This is post hitching post
This is post death
This is post metaphor
This is post truth
This is post communication
This is post thinking animals
This is post science
This is post possibility
This is post ending
This is post thinking about death

This is post importance
This is post big lessons in literature
This is post coding
This is post philosophy
This is post feminism
This is post colony collapse disorder
Not post bees

Walk in Song

for Christi Belcourt

on the path of vamps
every step, unfinished lives
of sisters, cousins, aunties, mothers,
grandmothers and great-great grandmothers

an emotional footprint
acknowledges hundreds of years
of intricate beadwork: feathers,
moon cycles, eagle eyes,
baby feet, plants, rivers,
a kaleidoscope of colours
embody stolen beings

yellow emergency tape:
Police Line Do Not Cross
and *Hello My Name Is: Who Cares*
confronts ongoing genocide

brown skin angels, little girls
tug on buckskin dress
three generations of women,
grandmother holds daughter,
who carries baby
strapped to her back

a mermaid with long black
hair swims, *singing*
part mythology, all spirit

generations of ancestors weep
through every honour song

Red Dress Chant

Redress a roaring
land

Redress the ocean
uprising
Redress out
side her house
Redress an exploding sunrise

Redress released power

Redress beadwork so detailed you can't dismiss

Redress strength after contact
Redress a voice connected

Redress a shift
ing narrative

Redress seeking understanding

Redress singing in ancestral languages

Redress dancing   with Creator

Redress a   winter rising

Redress spirit

in motion

Redress generations

of women

Redress unwavering family love

Redress unforgettable

luminosity

Redress identity's revelation

This Silent Generation

I want to be your powwow grounds
                        all that is worth protecting.

                Pay attention; I'm your radiant gathering.

Know the rhythm of your heart
                        trust wherever

spirit wants to go.

Fill minds with voices of ancestors.

                Sing broken prayers for sunless skies.

If anyone has arrived or mastered grace

                        pardon death, and receive your rewards

my lament for a universal kingdom.

                Give rest to graciousness.   Make love real.

                        Set yourself free.
Hide in the folds.

                        Stretch your hand over the sea.

Architect of Desire

"a woman's sex is as sacred as her land"
—*Gwen Benaway*

Your kisses are formations

no design could ever touch.

You guide like a sanctuary
no drafts of penance

only plans to worship.

I Returned My Bones to the Ocean's Body

You held my clothes on stolen land. Witnessed ceremony.

You shed my feathers on Sturgeon Full Moon, spooned me on grandfather rocks, and kissed the insides of my wrists. You carried me through dark nights when new moon forgot to show.

You took my hand as we walked on Mi'kmaki's Ripening Moon. We called it when the Mate Called Her Moon. I returned to you at the meeting place at harvest with Hunter's lunar light. You rushed back to me as Moon River froze. Now we await Creator's decolonial orchestra in a primitive hut.

This is our practice. Our love is unlearning. Our only living treaty.

Water

Amisisguapua'q. Elasugwet. A'sugwesugwigij. Asoqomasugwet. Gesigawitg. Getapa'q. Esamqwat. Gjigapa'n. Gta'n. Jipu'ji'j. Lampo'q. Lapaltnewel. Magatgwig.

Water is an ancient realm. Water intervenes and connects. Water is movement and history. Water holds and protects. Water releases and bombards. Water is ecology and future. Water traumatizes and witnesses. Water silences. Water resolves. Water is absent and violent. Water survives. Water is wound and healer. Water speaks.

Wela'lioq water protectors. Wela'lin.

We are made of oceans. We are made of inaudible waterways. We are volatile undercurrents. We are upstream. We are replenishing downstream. We are rushing rivers. We are winding waterfalls. We are overflowing lakes. We are wayward waterways. We are wild swimmers. We are liquid ceremony. We are sky. We are vapour. We are unnameable fluidity. We are pollution in the sea. We are languages of saliva. We are bodies of water.

Notes to the Poems

In "Letter to Joseph R. Smallwood," I draw on
A Really Good Brown Girl by Marilyn Dumont
(Brick Books, 1996).

In "The Antelope's Wife," I draw on The
Antelope's Wife by Louise Erdrich (Flamingo,
1998).

In "Architect of Desire," I draw on Holy Wild by
Gwen Benaway (Book*hug, 2018).

In "Water," I draw on Mi'gmaq-Mi'kmaq Online
(www.mikmaqonline.org).

Afterword

THE SEVEN SACRED TEACHINGS ARE the guiding principles of Indigenous ways of being. In the Mi'kmaq culture, the Seven Sacred Teachings are associated with the seven stages of life, which are broken into four life transitions. At thirty-five years old, I'm coming into the era of life where my spiritual awareness becomes more realized. I am learning to walk with love, respect, bravery, honesty, humility, truth, and hopefully wisdom.

Life makes significant changes in seven-year cycles.

In 2011, I was sent a confirmation from Indian and Northern Affairs Canada of registration as an "Indian and as a member of the Qalipu Mi'kmaq First Nation." My registration number is 0341945201.

At this time, Qalipu (the Mi'kmaw word for caribou) was known as the landless band because it's one of the few First Nations bands without a reservation. In returning to this collection of poetry and landing on a title, I wanted it to represent this revisioned work, as well as speak back to this misperception of landlessness.

No one in Ktaqamkuk (the Mi'kmaw word for Newfoundland, which translates to land across water) is landless. Exactly seven years later, I've been issued yet another document from Indigenous and Northern Affairs, which notes my removal from the Indian Register.

"I regret to inform you that, since your name does not appear on the updated Founding Members List, you are no longer entitled for registration in accordance with paragraph 6(1)(b) of the Indian Act and your name has been deleted from the Indian Register accordingly."

Whether my name appears on a register ever again, I know who I am, and to whom I belong, and that my ancestors are always with me. My work is to honour seven generations before, and after. I want readers to know *I Am a Body of Land* is not a defence, but poetics of resistance and resilience.

An afterword is rarely written by the author of a text. Typically, an author outside of the work offers insight to close the book. Everything about the process of revising this work doesn't fit the typical literary way of doing things, and therefore breaks any previous rules or established means of production. This isn't traditional publishing, and rightly so. Indigenous poetry isn't stereotypical, or prescriptive. This isn't a typical book.

As the author of *I Am a Body of Land*, I would like to acknowledge the importance of taking ownership and accountability for the mistakes made leading up to the original publication of *Who Took My Sister?* A book that came out of an urgent sense of love, solidarity, and advocacy, but despite good intentions failed deeply.

For readers who are unaware, the initial publication of *Who Took My Sister?* was pulled several days after its publication on spring equinox. As my editor, Julie Joosten, and publishers Jay MillAr and Hazel Millar at Book*hug and I came to understand, we had made a major error. We had not asked permission from the families, or consulted with the various Indigenous communities involved in the text.

Despite the various complexities surrounding the work, the collection was taken out of circulation, and was no longer a promoted title. Many of these poems appeared in various literary journals, anthologies, and magazines, including the *Malahat Review, Canadian Literature, IMPACT: Colonialism in Canada, Arc Poetry Magazine, Riddle Fence*, and *Geist Magazine*, prior to the book's official publication. The poems were edited by Indigenous and non-Indigenous editors.

During the following months, Book*hug and I sent letters of apology to the four families whose loved ones appeared in the original text, and we are grateful for the responses we received. To these families—and anyone who experienced pain or trauma because of the sensitive nature of material included in *Who Took My Sister?*—I remain deeply sorry and continue to offer my sincere apologies.

While poetry has long been a form of elegy, it does not honour a person's life to create another gravestone. The last thing I ever wanted to do was create more harm, yet can now recognize the poetics did not belong to me; they weren't mine to write. One cannot confess to understand or know, let alone write, another person's trauma. To align yourself with trauma beyond your own lived experience is problematic, and perhaps even dangerous.

Honour comes from a living place.

Ideally, as a writer I would have come up in community and learned about Indigenous protocol prior to the initial publication of the poems. But due to the complexities of colonization and displacement, I am learning and unlearning as I go, sometimes publicly, and perhaps even with great humiliation and naïveté.

In revising this collection of poetry under the guidance of

Lee Maracle, I have learned more than I can articulate, and am deeply humbled by her teachings and grateful for her generosity as a guide.

As Lee noted in her introduction, I don't want to ever end up back on her porch revising my poetry. This being said, I would welcome any other opportunity to sit with Lee, as her laughter, stories, and lessons resonate eternally. She is a remarkable gift of a writer, reader, and exceptional editor. Working with Lee has changed my way of seeing the world and, in turn, my work as a poet.

Throughout this process, I've shared several conversations with Gregory Younging, whose book *Elements of Indigenous Style: A Guide for Writing By and About Indigenous Peoples* has been instrumental. I remain deeply appreciative of his ongoing generosity, compassion, and teachings. I will carry the principle of "do no more harm" forward in my writing practice.

And finally, I would like to acknowledge this new text, *I Am a Body of Land*, as a poetic attempt to undo harm and repair relations. It's an offering—a collection of poems within a book of poems about finding and honouring spirit. Like the author of this work, these poems contain multitudes. Wela'lin for your patience, reader. May the work honour. Msit No'Kmaq.

Shannon Webb-Campbell
October 2018

(Land) Ackowledgements

I am infinitely grateful to the ancestors, my families, especially my mother, Diane Campbell, and father, Kevin Webb, who continue to support. My step-parents, Graham Campbell, Mary Jean Clark, and Des Hawley, and my ever-expanding cast of siblings, nieces, and nephews, and animal family. Wela'lin to my love, Andrew Gray, my friends, rivers, stars, moon phases, ponds, Northern Lights, birds, leaves, oceans, crows, mountains, fish, and lands where I've been able to live, gather, and write on Turtle Island, especially Mi'kma'ki, Ktaqamkuk, and Mohawk territory.

A very special thank-you to Lee Maracle, both for the day on the porch and all her teachings. To Jay MillAr and Hazel Millar at Book*hug, and Julie Joosten, who helped carry this book through an important editorial process. Wela'lin to knowledge keepers Cal White and Gregory Younging.

I am humbled by my readers and fellow poets Carol Rose Daniels, Rosanna Deerchild, and Susan Musgrave, who generously took time and care to read the work.

Thank you to the artists, writers, poets, academics, and activists for the ongoing conversations beyond these pages. I see you, and your work.

May we all honour these traditional lands and waters, and tread lightly for the next seven generations.

Shannon Webb-Campbell is a mixed-Indigenous (Mi'kmaq) settler poet, writer, and critic currently based in Montreal. Her first book, *Still No Word* (2015) was the inaugural recipient of Egale Canada's Out In Print Award. She was Canadian Women in the Literary Arts Critic-in-Residence in 2014, and sits on Canadian Women in the Literary Arts board of directors. Her work has appeared in many anthologies, journals and publications across Canada including *The Globe and Mail*, *Geist Magazine*, *The Malahat Review*, *Canadian Literature*, *Room*, and *Quill and Quire*. In 2017 she facilitated a book club-style reading of *The Final Report of the Truth and Reconciliation Commission of Canada* at Atwater Library in Montreal; she also championed Carol Daniel's novel *Bearskin Diary* for CBC Montreal's Turtle Island Reads. *I Am a Body of Land* is her latest book.

Colophon

Manufactured as the first edition of *I Am a Body of Land* in the spring of 2019 by Book*hug Press.

Edited for the press by Lee Maracle
Copy edited by Stuart Ross
Cover design by Tree Abraham
Typeset by Jay MillAr